Flute

Alfred's INSTRUMENTAL CD PLAY-ALONG

Classic Rock
INSTRUMENTAL SOLOS

THE SPENCER DAVIS GROUP

EAGLES

FLEETWOOD MAC

the rolling stones

JOURNEY

LED ZEPPELIN

Chicago

Cream

norman greenbaum

Wilson Pickett

YES

Arranged by Bill Galliford, Ethan Neuburg and Tod Edmondson

© 2011 Alfred Music Publishing Co., Inc.
All Rights Reserved. Printed in USA.

ISBN-10: 0-7390-7991-3
ISBN-13: 978-0-7390-7991-1

Alfred

Alfred Cares. Contents printed on 100% recycled paper.

Contents

GIMME SOME LOVIN'

Track 2: Demo
Track 3: Play Along

Words and Music by
STEVE WINWOOD, MUFF WINWOOD
and SPENCER DAVIS

Moderately fast rock (♩ = 144)

25 OR 6 TO 4

Track 4: Demo
Track 5: Play Along

Words and Music by
ROBERT LAMM

Moderately bright rock (♩ = 144)

GO YOUR OWN WAY

Track 6: Demo
Track 7: Play Along

Moderately bright rock (♩ = 136)

Words and Music by
LINDSEY BUCKINGHAM

HOTEL CALIFORNIA

Track 8: Demo
Track 9: Play Along

Words and Music by
DON HENLEY, GLENN FREY
and DON FELDER

Hotel California - 3 - 1

ROUNDABOUT

Track 10: Demo
Track 11: Play Along

Words and Music by
JON ANDERSON and STEVE HOWE

Roundabout - 3 - 1

11

Roundabout - 3 - 3

IN THE MIDNIGHT HOUR

Track 12: Demo
Track 13: Play Along

Words by
WILSON PICKETT

Music by
STEVE CROPPER

In the Midnight Hour - 2 - 1

OPEN ARMS

Track 14: Demo
Track 15: Play Along

Words and Music by
JONATHAN CAIN and STEVE PERRY

Slowly, expressively (♩ = 96)

(I CAN'T GET NO) SATISFACTION

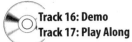
Track 16: Demo
Track 17: Play Along

Words and Music by
MICK JAGGER and KEITH RICHARDS

Moderately, driving (♩ = 132)

STAIRWAY TO HEAVEN

Track 18: Demo
Track 19: Play Along

Words and Music by
JIMMY PAGE and ROBERT PLANT

SPIRIT IN THE SKY

Track 20: Demo
Track 21: Play Along

Words and Music by
NORMAN GREENBAUM

Moderate blues shuffle (♩ = 128) (♫ = ♩♪³)

*C♭ = B♮

Spirit in the Sky - 2 - 1

DON'T STOP BELIEVIN'

Track 22: Demo
Track 23: Play Along

Words and Music by
JONATHAN CAIN, NEAL SCHON
and STEVE PERRY

Don't Stop Believin' - 2 - 1

Don't Stop Believin' - 2 - 2

SUNSHINE OF YOUR LOVE

Track 24: Demo
Track 25: Play Along

Words and Music by
JACK BRUCE, PETE BROWN
and ERIC CLAPTON

PARTS OF A FLUTE AND FINGERING CHART

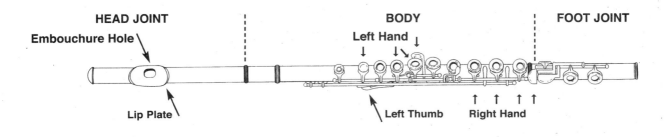

● = press the key.
○ = do not press the key.

When there are two fingerings given for a note, use the first one unless the alternate fingering is suggested.

When two enharmonic notes are given together (F♯ and G♭ as an example), they sound the same pitch and are played the same way.

INSTRUMENTAL SOLOS

This instrumental series contains themes from **Blizzard Entertainment's** popular massively multiplayer online role-playing game and includes 4 pages of art from the World of Warcraft universe. The compatible arrangements are carefully edited for the Level 2-3 player, and include an accompaniment CD which features a demo track and play-along track. Titles: Lion's Pride • The Shaping of the World • Pig and Whistle • Slaughtered Lamb • Invincible • A Call to Arms • Gates of the Black Temple • Salty Sailor • Wrath of the Lich King • Garden of Life.

(00-36626) | Flute Book & CD | $12.99

(00-36629) | Clarinet Book & CD | $12.99

(00-36632) | Alto Sax Book & CD | $12.99

(00-36635) | Tenor Sax Book & CD | $12.99

(00-36638) | Trumpet Book & CD | $12.99

(00-36641) | Horn in F Book & CD | $12.99

(00-36644) | Trombone Book & CD | $12.99

(00-36647) | Piano Acc. Book & CD | $14.99

(00-36650) | Violin Book & CD | $16.99

(00-36653) | Viola Book & CD | $16.99

(00-36656) | Cello Book & CD | $16.99